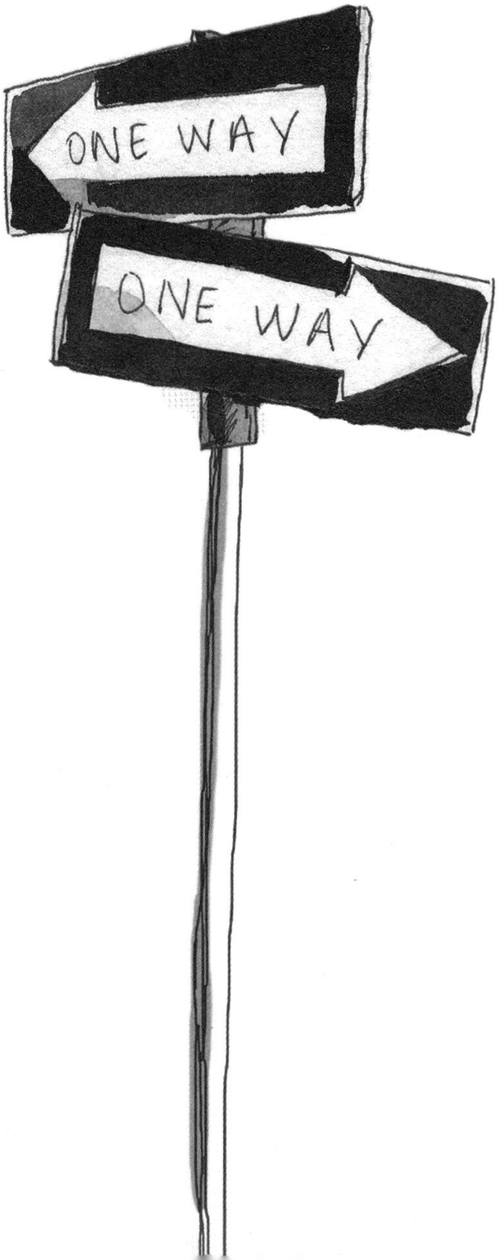
ONE WAY
ONE WAY

750cc DOWN LINCOLN HIGHWAY

WRITER: **Bernard CHAMBAZ**
ART: **BARROUX**

nbm GRAPHIC NOVELS
Nantier • Beall • Minoustchine
NEW YORK

ISBN 9781681122458
Library of Congress Control Number: 2019954402
© 2018 URBAN COMICS, by Chambaz, Barroux
© 2020 NBM for the English translation
Translation by Joe Johnson
Lettering by Ortho
First printing January 2020

Available also wherever ebooks are sold

VERRAZZANO BRIDGE

i HATE THE MARATHON.

I HATE RUNNING.

AN HOUR BEFORE THE START, I GOT A TEXT. INSTEAD OF "GOOD LUCK," IT SAID "WE'RE FINISHED."

SO, I WENT TO A BAR NEXT TO THE SUBWAY ON 96TH. HAD A FEW BOURBONS WITH SOME OTHER MOPE.

ONE TO HER HEALTH, A SECOND ONE TO MYSELF FOR CONSOLATION, AND A THIRD TO THAT OF MY NEIGHBOR.

ED TOLD ME HIS LIFE STORY. I TOLD HIM ONLY THAT MY GIRLFRIEND HAD JUST DUMPED ME. HE EVIDENTLY HAD EXPERIENCE WITH THAT. HE ORDERED TWO MORE BOURBONS.

HIS PHILOSOPHY COULD BE SUMMED UP IN TWO, RATHER EASILY UNDERSTOOD, PRINCIPLES. FIRST, YOU FORGET HER! SECOND, YOU TAKE OFF!

MANHATTAN

I DON'T KNOW WHETHER IT WAS ED OR ME WHO GOT THE IDEA.

ED'S THE ONE WHO TOLD ME ABOUT LINCOLN. ABRAHAM LINCOLN, THE 16TH PRESIDENT OF THE UNITED STATES OF AMERICA. ED'S THE ONE WHO TOLD ME ABOUT THE LINCOLN HIGHWAY, THE ROAD CROSSING THE USA FROM THE EAST COAST TO THE WEST COAST.

I'M THE ONE WHO THOUGHT OF THE MOTORCYCLE. I RESERVED A SHADOW 750 FOR THE NEXT MORNING. I DRANK A FEW MORE BOURBONS.

THAT NIGHT, I TRIED TO SLEEP. BETWEEN JETLAG AND GHOSTS OF MY GIRLFRIEND, IT WASN'T EASY.

HUDSON RIVER

THE LIGHT TUMBLES DOWN BETWEEN THE BLOCKS OF SKYSCRAPERS. I BOARD THE FERRY. THE FIRST MILE'S DONE NOW! ONLY 3,388 TO GO!

I DIDN'T CHOOSE THE COLOR OF THE SHADOW, BUT I DO LIKE IT. ALONG WITH THE OPEN-FACE HELMET, I GOT AVIATOR SUNGLASSES. I PACKED CLOTHING, ROADMAPS, AND THE MAINTENANCE INSTRUCTIONS IN THE SADDLEBAGS.

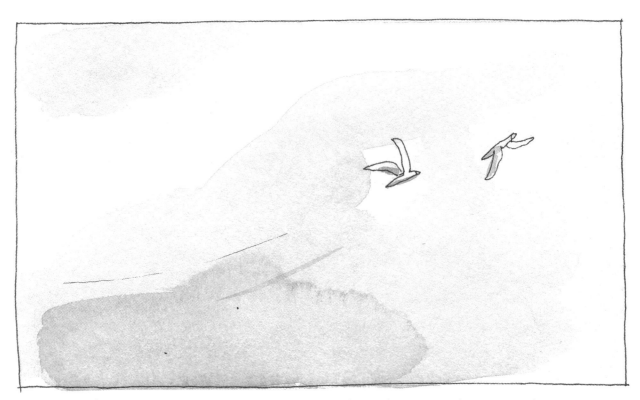

THE CAPTAIN ANNOUNCES THAT THE HUDSON RIVER IS AN ANCIENT GLACIAL FJORD
AND THAT ITS WATERS ORIGINATE IN LAKE "TEAR OF THE CLOUDS."

I TELL MYSELF I DID WELL TO COME THIS WAY.

WEEHAWKEN

HERE'S WHERE FRED ASTAIRE BEGAN DANCING, BUT FRANKLY, THAT DOESN'T LIGHTEN MY MOOD.

YOU CAN EASILY FIND YOUR WAY. ROUTE 27 FIRST HEADS WEST THEN SOUTH. THE SKY IS GRAY. FOR THE MOMENT, THAT DOESN'T BOTHER ME. THE ROAD IS DRY. IT'S BETTER FOR GETTING STARTED.

PRINCETON

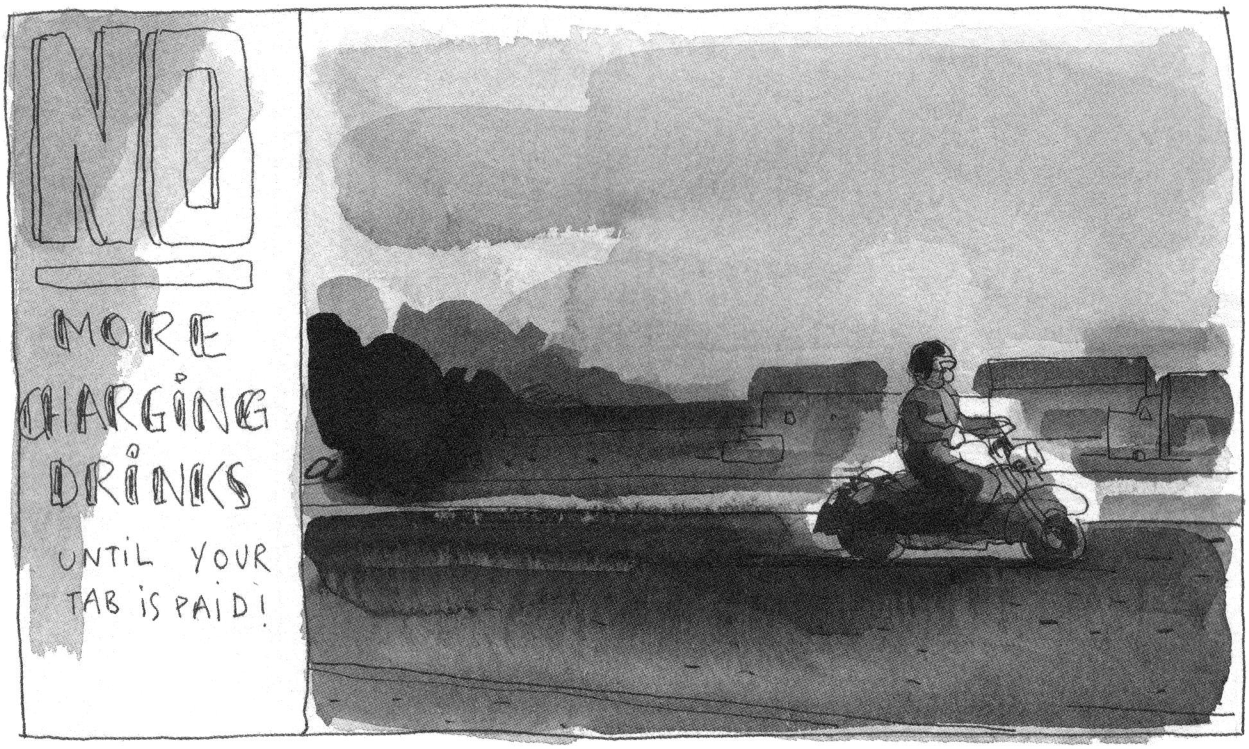
NO
MORE
CHARGING
DRINKS
UNTIL YOUR
TAB IS PAID!

A BREAK WOULD BE WELCOME. NOT TO REST, BECAUSE I'VE ALWAYS LOVED RIDING WITHOUT STOPPING, BUT TO HAVE A DRINK, BECAUSE I'M THIRSTY.

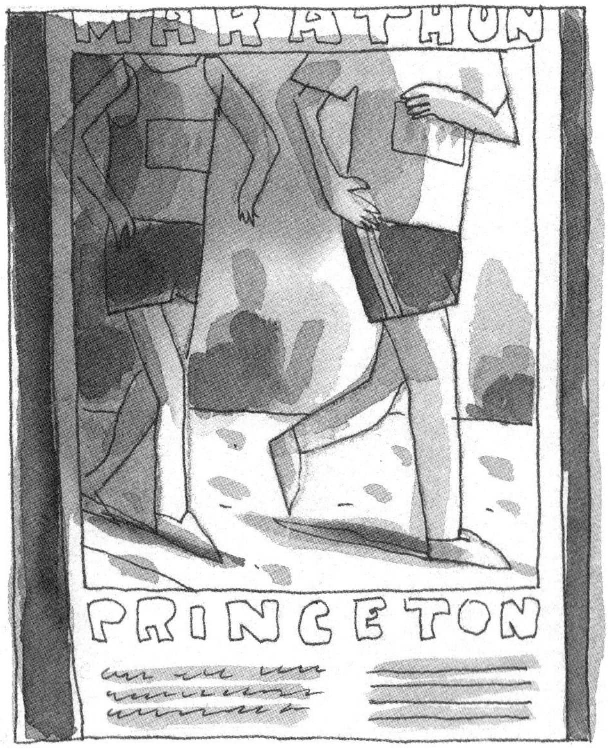
MARATHON
PRINCETON

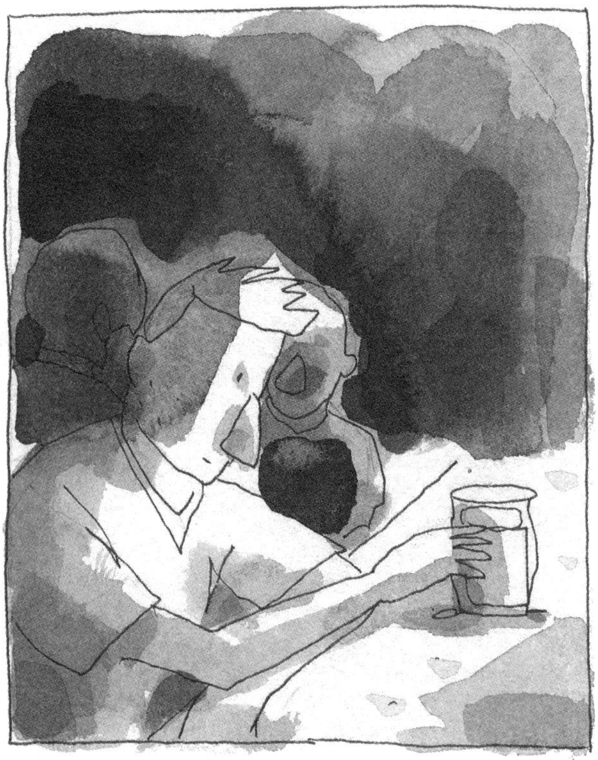

PRINCETON SEEMS LIKE A PLEASANT CITY. AT THE ENTRANCE OF THE UNIVERSITY CAMPUS, A BANNER ANNOUNCES A SEMI-MARATHON. "THE BIGGEST THING TO HIT PRINCETON SINCE THE BIG BANG." I PREFER TO DRINK MY BEER A LITTLE FARTHER ALONG.

TRENTON

ON THE METAL BRIDGE SPANNING THE DELAWARE RIVER CAN BE READ "TRENTON MAKES, THE WORLD TAKES," WHICH RECALLS THE GOOD OLD DAYS OF RUBBER AND CIGARS.

AT THE END OF THE DAY, WITH A LITTLE LUCK, YOU CAN SEE THE SHADOW OF A WHITE WHALE. CLEARLY, THIS ISN'T A LUCKY TIME FOR ME.

THE FIRST MOTEL TO COME ALONG IS FINE. AFTER A HAWAIIAN PIZZA, I BUY MYSELF TWO GLASSES OF BOURBON. THE FIRST ONE TO ED'S HEALTH. THE SECOND TO MINE.

THEN I GO BACK UPSTAIRS TO MY ROOM. I STRETCH OUT ON MY BED. THE WORLD HAS SLOWED DOWN. I THINK IT MOVED A LITTLE BIT AGAIN, AND THEN IT STOPPED.

LANGHORNE

I'D BARELY HEADED OUT WHEN I HEARD A REPEATED NOISE. "NOISE" IS AN OVERSTATEMENT. "CLICKING" WOULD BE MORE PRECISE. I SLOW DOWN TO TRY TO FIGURE OUT WHERE IT WAS COMING FROM. EVEN IF I DO, I WON'T BE ANY BETTER OFF.

AT THE ENTRANCE TO LANGHORNE, I GET LUCKY: "LINCOLN GARAGE," WRITTEN IN BLACK LETTERS ON A BEIGE FACADE THAT LOOKS LIKE A MOVIE SET. IT'S GOOD TIMING. THE MECHANIC HAS AN ITALIAN NAME AND KNOWS MOTORCYCLES. MY TIMING'S EVEN BETTER. IT JUST NEEDED TUNING. NO PROB.

PHILADELPHIA

HERE'S WHERE THE DECLARATION OF INDEPENDENCE WAS SIGNED. NOWADAYS, IT'S WHERE THEY HOLD THE "WING BOWL," WHICH CONSISTS OF GOBBLING DOWN THE GREATEST NUMBER OF CHICKEN WINGS. THE WINNER EATS TWO HUNDRED AND FIFTY-FIVE. ROMAN EMPERORS ARE ASTRIDE STAGE FLOATS AND A DEVIL STRADDLES A CARDBOARD COFFIN.

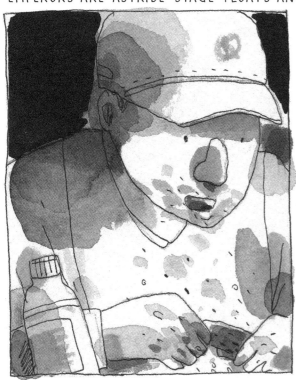

EXHILIRATED SPECTATORS WHO HAVE RESERVED THE TWENTY THOUSAND SEATS SEVERAL MONTHS IN ADVANCE, GREET, WITH WAR CRIES, THE BIKINI-CLAD COHOSTS STRUTTING AROUND AMID A GROUP OF HE-MEN DRESSED UP AS SUPERMAN.

AT CARIBOU COFFEE ON WALNUT STREET, I GET MYSELF A SECOND BREAKFAST. NO CHICKEN WINGS OR COHOSTS IN BIKINIS. THE WAITRESS HAS A TIRED, PRETTY SMILE. I ORDER A COFFEE FROM HER THAT'S NOT BAD AND A SERVING OF CHEESECAKE THAT'LL DO ME GOOD.

IN THE BACK OF THE CAFE, A GUY IS SPENDING HIS TIME LAUGHING ON HIS CELLPHONE. I DON'T REGRET THROWING MINE OUT THE WINDOW LAST NIGHT.

PARADISE

AFTER A SHORT HOUR ON HIGHWAY 1, I HAVE TO TAKE HIGHWAY 30 AND I'M HAPPY TO LEARN I'LL STAY ON IT FOR SEVERAL DAYS. PARADISE IS THE NAME OF A SMALL TOWN. FOR ALL THAT IT'S NOT IDYLLIC, IT HAS A PRETTY NAME AND THAT'S NOT A BAD START.

INCIDENTALLY, THE COUNTY MUST BE UNDER THE CONTROL OF POETS OR OPTIMISTS, ONE OR THE OTHER, BECAUSE THERE'S ALSO A "MOUNT JOY" AND "BIRD-IN-HAND" NEARBY.

GETTYSBURG

HERE I AM IN FRONT OF THE MOST FAMOUS FIELD OF BATTLE FROM THE CIVIL WAR.
THERE ARE THOUSANDS OF TOMBSTONES TOPPED WITH LITTLE AMERICAN FLAGS,
ALONG WITH CANNONS AND MANNEQUINS IN UNIFORMS,

WITH FIELDS AND WOODS ON THE HORIZON, SCATTERED SCULPTURES, VISITORS.

"IT IS FOR US THE LIVING, RATHER, TO BE DEDICATED HERE TO THE UNFINISHED WORK WHICH THEY WHO FOUGHT HERE HAVE THUS FAR SO NOBLY ADVANCED. IT IS RATHER FOR US TO BE HERE DEDICATED TO THE GREAT TASK REMAINING BEFORE US -- THAT FROM THESE HONORED DEAD WE TAKE INCREASED DEVOTION TO THAT CAUSE FOR WHICH THEY GAVE THE LAST FULL MEASURE OF DEVOTION -- THAT WE HERE HIGHLY RESOLVE THAT THESE DEAD SHALL NOT HAVE DIED IN VAIN -- THAT THIS NATION, UNDER GOD, SHALL HAVE A NEW BIRTH OF FREEDOM -- AND THAT GOVERNMENT OF THE PEOPLE, BY THE PEOPLE, FOR THE PEOPLE, SHALL NOT PERISH FROM THE EARTH."

HERE ARE 108 OF THE 272 WORDS THAT LINCOLN SPOKE HERE, BESIDE MY SHADOW, AND WHICH BILL KNOWS BY HEART.

BESIDE MY SHADOW, A GUY ON A HARLEY THROTTLES THE GAS AND LOWERS THE KICKSTAND. BILL'S WEARING AN ORANGE LEATHER VEST AND A BANDANA. HE'S GOING THE OTHER WAY. HE'S HEADING EAST TOWARDS THE OCEAN. HE ASKS ME WHERE I'M COMING FROM AND WHERE I'M GOING.

HE DOESN'T ASK ME WHY. I'D HAVE FOUND A GOOD REASON TO GIVE HIM ANYWAY. HE KNOWS THE ROAD ALL THE WAY TO CHICAGO. HE SAYS IT'S COOL.

FAYETTEVILLE

IT SEEMS THERE ARE TEN FAYETTEVILLES IN THE USA. BUT THERE'S ONLY ONE IN PENNSYLVANIA. THERE'S ALSO A LAFAYETTE. SINCE I'M IN FAYETTEVILLE, I LOOK FOR A STATUE OF LA FAYETTE. WHEN I ASK, THE ANSWER'S ALWAYS THE SAME.

NOBODY KNOWS, APART FROM A HELPFUL GUY IN A PICKUP WHO TELLS ME TO FOLLOW HIM, BUT WHO LEADS ME TO THE HONDA DEALERSHIP.

MY MOTEL RESEMBLES ALL MOTELS. BEFORE DINNER, i FELT A VAGUE NEED TO RUN, BUT i SENSED i WASN'T READY YET.

AT TWO IN THE MORNING, i FINALLY TURN OFF THE TV.

MOUNT ARARAT

THE ROAD IS CLIMBING AMID THE PINE TREES. A BIG SWITCHBACK HERALDS THE SUMMIT. I LEAN THE MOTORCYCLE INTO THE CURVE AND ACCELERATE AS I COME OUT OF IT. UP TOP, A SIGN INDICATES THAT WE'RE AT 2,464 FEET IN ALTITUDE.

OF COURSE, THERE'S NO SNOW OR GLACIER, NO ICE CREAM SHOP EITHER. WHY STOP?

A FELLOW RIDER GREETS ME. FIVE YEARS AGO, HE CAME TO SPREAD HIS FATHER'S ASHES HERE. EVERY YEAR, HE MAKES A RETURN TRIP. I TELL HIM SIMPLY, JUST TO SAY SOMETHING AND ALSO BECAUSE I'M THINKING IT, THAT THE OLD MAN MUST BE HAPPY.

HE SHOWS ME A PHOTO OF HIS FATHER IN FRONT OF THE S.S. GRAND VIEW POINT HOTEL, A MAN IN A PLAID SHIRT, IN THE PRIME OF LIFE. NAT LIVES IN PITTSBURGH. HE OFFERS TO RIDE ALONG WITH ME.

TURTLE CREEK

TURTLE CREEK IS A RIVER'S NAME. THERE WERE PROBABLY TURTLES IN THE AREA. IN ANY CASE, THE IROQUOIS WERE THE FIRST ONES TO GIVE NAMES TO RIVERS IN THE AREA. WE STOP FOR AN HOUR.

BACK ON HIS MOTORCYCLE, NAT RUNS HIS MOTOR FOR A GOOD WHILE BEFORE TAKING OFF AGAIN, AND HE LISTENS TO THE CYLINDERS LIKE THEY WERE A PERCUSSION CONCERT. I LET HIM LEAD THE WAY. HE RIDES SLOWLY. THE WEATHER IS DIVINE.

PITTSBURGH

IT'S STUCK WITH THE REPUTATION OF BEING A DIRTY CITY FILLED WITH SMOKE FROM STEEL MILLS. NOWADAYS, IT SEEMS THE CITY IS RANKED AMONG THE BEST CITIES FOR ITS QUALITY OF LIFE. AMERICANS LOVE RANKINGS. THEY'VE ALSO RANKED IT AS ONE OF THE CLOUDIEST CITIES IN THE COUNTRY. IN THAT RESPECT, I'M LUCKY.

NAT HAS SET UP A VEGETABLE GARDEN ON TOP OF HIS HOUSE'S ROOF. HE GROWS TOMATOES AND BEANS, AND WOULD HAPPILY GROW A FOOT OR TWO OF POT. THAT EVENING, HE SUGGESTS GOING OUT. I PREFER TO STAY STRETCHED OUT ON A CHAISE LONGUE, AMID THE TOMATOES AND STARS.

WEST VIRGINIA

BEFORE YOU EVEN FINISH READING THE SIGN "WELCOME TO WEST VIRGINIA", YOU FIND THE ONE "LEAVING WEST VIRGINIA." IT'S ONLY 5 MILES. BUT IT IS ONE OF 13 STATES THIS HIGHWAY GOES THROUGH.

SHE'S FAMOUS FOR THE SCENERY, THE COMFORT FOOD, SOUTHERN COOKING. I HAVE TO KEEP MOVING THOUGH. THE SKY IS GETTING CLOUDY AND THREATENING.

EAST LIVERPOOL

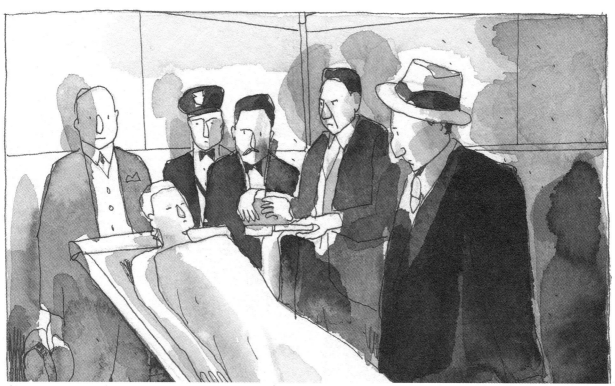

NAT RECOMMENDED TO ME A SMALL, SIX-ROOM HOTEL, THE "STURGIS HOUSE," A VICTORIAN WITH A PORCH. THAT'S WHERE THE CORPSE OF "PRETTY BOY FLOYD" WAS SHAVED, EMBALMED, AND DISPLAYED ON OCTOBER 22, 1934. AFTER PURSUING HIM FOR THREE DAYS, FBI AGENTS SHOT HIM DOWN IN A CORNFIELD. HE GAVE UP THE GHOST UNDER

AN APPLE TREE. ARRESTED FOR HAVING ROBBED BANKS AND FOR VAGRANCY, "PRETTY BOY" WAS GENEROUS TOWARDS THE POOR AND HAD EARNED THE NICKNAME "ROBIN HOOD." BEFORE GOING BACK INTO MY ROOM, I SALUTE HIS PLASTER DEATH MASK HANGING ON THE HALLWAY WALL.

OHIO

DAPPLED SKIES LAST NO LONGER THAN MADE-UP WOMEN. THE OLD PEOPLE WERE RIGHT. IN THE GUISE OF AN INDIAN SUMMER, THE CLOUDS HAVE BROUGHT RAIN. BUT I'M LIKE COUNTRY-FOLK, I LIKE THE RAIN.

ON THE MOTORCYCLE, WITH WATERPROOF VEST AND PANTS, YOU'RE STILL THE KING OF THE WORLD. YOU JUST HAVE TO BRAKE SOONER AND MORE GENTLY. THE ROAD'S A MARVELOUS, GLISTENING RIBBON RIGHT THEN.

CANTON

THE RAIN DOESN'T LET UP. IT'S LIKE I'M IN A BUBBLE. THE ROAD SHINES. IN THE END, I GIVE MYSELF A LONG STOPOVER, A NICE ONE. IF I'D STOPPED AT CANTON, I COULD'VE VISITED THE MCKINLEY MUSEUM, NAMED FOR THE PRESIDENT OF THE USA ASSASSINATED BY AN ANARCHIST IN 1901.

I DIDN'T UNDERSTAND WHETHER HE'D ALREADY GONE TO SEE THE NIAGARA FALLS OR IF HE WAS GOING TO SEE THEM WHEN HE GOT TWO BULLETS IN HIS ABDOMEN. THE ROAD IS STRAIGHT, THE SKY STRETCHES OVER THE ROAD.

VAN WERT

I'M HEADING TOWARDS VAN WERT, THE PEONY CAPITAL. TWO HUNDREDS MILES IN ONE SHOT, APART FROM STOPPING FOR A FILL-UP AND A CUP OF COFFEE.

MONOTONY DOESN'T BOTHER ME. OTHERWISE, I WOULDN'T HAVE RUN FOR HOURS AND HOURS TO COMPETE IN MARATHONS.

ZULU

I'D BEEN WONDERING WHAT ZULU WOULD BE LIKE. WELL, ZULU LOOKS LIKE ANY TINY AMERICAN TOWN. THERE'S NOTHING AFRICAN ABOUT IT, EXCEPT FOR A TALL, VERY SKINNY BLACK MAN SWEEPING THE FORECOURT OF THE PRESBYTERIAN CHURCH.

I'M RIDING AGAIN UNDER A TIMID SUN. I'M HAPPY TO LEARN INDIANA IS THE LAND OF THE TRUMPET AND HAZELNUTS.

FORT WAYNE

IT'S BEEN FIVE DAYS SINCE I SET OUT. MY SADNESS IS FADING BIT BY BIT. BUT MY LACK OF UNDERSTANDING REMAINS. IN ANY CASE, I DON'T HAVE ANY CLEAN CLOTHES. I GO TO THE LAUNDROMAT. I WAIT PATIENTLY ALONG WITH TACITURN MEXICAN WORKERS AND A PRETTY YOUNG WOMAN TO WHOM I DON'T DARE UTTER A WORD.

WHEN SHE BENDS DOWN TO OPEN THE DOOR OF THE MACHINE, HER PONYTAIL FALLS INTO HER EYES, AND THE MOVEMENT SHE MAKES TO PUT IT BACK BEHIND HER HEAD WRENCHES MY HEART. WHEN I RETURN, I GIVE THE SHADOW 750 A WIPE DOWN.

WHAT'S THERE TO DO TONIGHT? THE DOWNTOWN IS DESERTED. THE BARS ARE EMPTY. I DON'T KNOW WHERE THE YOUNG WOMAN WITH THE PONYTAIL IS. THE ZOO IS CLOSED.

THE STAR ATTRACTION THERE WAS A HYENA, BUT IT HAS DIED FROM AN ILLNESS. THE REST IS PLEASANT ENOUGH: GIRAFFES, ZEBRAS, TIGERS, OWLS, AND A FEW SPECIES THAT ARE LESS COMMON LIKE BLACK-FOOTED PENGUINS. SO I THINK I'LL GO RUN.

MERRIAM

THIS IS THE FIRST NIGHT I'VE SLEPT WELL. A SHORT WHILE AFTER MY THREE WAFFLES WITH MAPLE SYRUP, I'M AT THE TOMB OF UNCLE SAM. THE TOMBSTONE IS TINY.

THEY'RE NOT ENTIRELY SURE IT'S HIM. WHATEVER THE CASE, THE DROPS OF DEW MAKE THE GRASS SPARKLE.

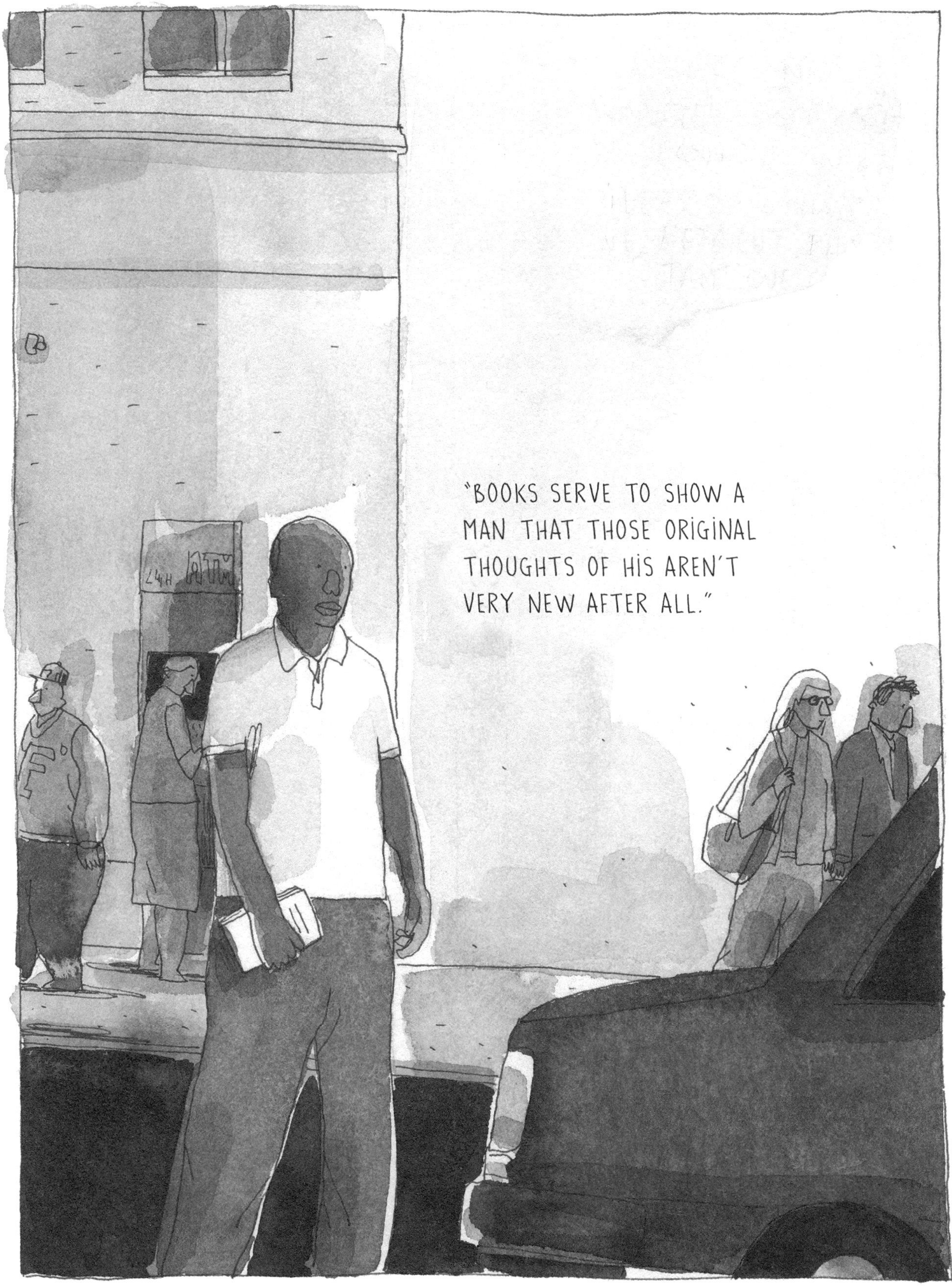
"BOOKS SERVE TO SHOW A MAN THAT THOSE ORIGINAL THOUGHTS OF HIS AREN'T VERY NEW AFTER ALL."
24H ATM

CHICAGO

I'D GOTTEN ACCUSTOMED TO HIGHWAY 30. I DON'T KNOW EXACTLY WHEN I LEFT IT, BUT I WENT THROUGH SUBURBS FOR A GOOD HOUR BEFORE FINDING MYSELF ON A SIX-LANE INTERSTATE FACING THE SKYLINE.

SO, I LET OFF ON THE GAS TO GET ME AN EYEFUL.

AT 5:00PM, I GO OUT TO STRETCH MY LEGS. I CHOOSE THE STREETS BENEATH THE "L." IN THE END, I CAN'T RESIST THE TEMPTATION: TWO GRILLED HOTDOGS, ONIONS, MUSTARD, MAYO. NEXT, I GO ON TO GRANT PARK, WHERE THE START AND FINISH IS OF THEIR MARATHON. NOWADAYS, IT'S NAMED THE "BANK OF AMERICA CHICAGO MARATHON."

BEFORE RETURNING TO THE HOTEL, I PAY FOR THE RIDE UP THE JOHN HANCOCK CENTER. FOR EIGHTEEN DOLLARS, THE ELEVATOR WILL DROP YOU OFF ON THE OBSERVATION DECK OF THE 94TH FLOOR IN THIRTY-NINE SECONDS.

THAT EVENING, i ORDER A WHISKY FOR A CHANGE FROM BOURBON. A WOMAN iN A WHITE DRESS iS SEATED AT THE NEiGHBORiNG TABLE, iN FRONT OF TWO EMPTY GLASSES, BUT SHE iS OBVIOUSLY ALONE. SHE HAS A SAD LOOK THAT ENCOURAGES ME TO SPEAK TO HER.

NEXT, i MORE OR LESS REMEMBER HOW WE GOT FROM THE 94TH FLOOR TO THE GROUND FLOOR OF THE JOHN HANCOCK CENTER, BUT NOT REALLY HOW SHE ENDED UP iN MY BED.

PLAINFIELD

GETTING OUT OF CHICAGO IS MORE COMPLICATED THAN GETTING IN THERE, AND LOOKING AT THE MAP IS NO BIG HELP. IT'S NO USE DRAWING STRAIGHT LINES, THAT'S NOT THE SHORTEST WAY. I END UP JOINING HIGHWAY 30 AGAIN IN PLAINFIELD.

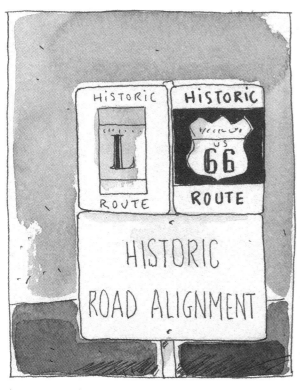

I'M SURPRISED TO LEARN SIMULTANEOUSLY THAT IT AND ROUTE 66 ARE THE SAME ROAD FOR THREE BLOCKS. THEN, I LET THE "MOTHER ROAD" HEAD ON SOUTH. I STAY ON THE "FATHER ROAD," HEADING DUE WEST. I'M A FAITHFUL KIND OF GUY.

DEKALB

IN THE MIDDLE OF TOWN, I PASS IN FRONT OF AN ART DECO BUILDING ADORNED WITH FRIEZES AND PHARAOH HEADS. IT'S A MOVIE THEATER, AND THAT MAY BE OSIRIS. HE WAS HEADING WEST EVERY DAY, TOO. IN PASSING, I RECOGNIZED THE POSTER FOR TITANIC.

BECAUSE OF THAT, I THINK BACK TO MY GIRLFRIEND'S TEXT: "WE'RE FINISHED." I STILL DON'T UNDERSTAND WHY.

MISSISSIPPI

YOU ANTICIPATE THE RIVER. YOU SENSE IT'S THERE BEFORE YOU SEE IT. IT'S EVEN WIDER THAN I'D IMAGINED. THE CURRENT IS STRONG IN PLACES, AND BITS OF WOOD FLOAT ALONG AT FULL TILT. JUST IN CASE, I LOOK TO SEE IF TOM SAWYER'S RAFT IS TIED TO A TREE ON THE RIVERBANK.

I'M NOT LIKELY TO SEE ANY FISH FROM THE BRIDGE. INSTEAD, I HAWK A BIG LOOGIE TOWARDS THE RIVER. I FEEL LIKE I'M PARTICIPATING IN THE VAST MOVEMENT OF CREATION AND THAT DOESN'T HURT A SOUL.

CLINTON

I LEAVE THE MISSISSIPPI BEHIND. EARLY THAT MORNING, PEOPLE ARE STANDING IN LINE ALONGSIDE A GYM. YOU MIGHT THINK THEY'VE COME TO BUY TICKETS FOR A BASKETBALL GAME, BUT THERE ARE LOTS OF KIDS, WOMEN, AND OLD FOLKS IN THE LINE, AND THEY DON'T LOOK HAPPY.

 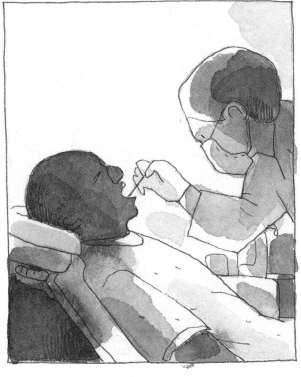

A BANNER REVEALS WHAT IT'S ALL ABOUT. VOLUNTEER DENTISTS HAVE COME TODAY TO GIVE FREE CARE TO A POPULATION LACKING NATIONAL HEALTHCARE.

"TACT IS THE ABILITY TO DESCRIBE OTHERS AS THEY SEE THEMSELVES."

THE ROAD FROM MECHANICSVILLE TO LISBON

I STOP IN FRONT OF AN ISOLATED HOUSE WITH A PERFECT LAWN. A MOTORCYCLE IS ON DISPLAY ON THE EDGE OF THE EMBANKMENT. THERE'S A SIGN WITH RED LETTERS ON THE SEAT. "FOR SALE." A GIGANTIC MAN SLOWLY APPROACHES. HE'S FORCED

TO SELL HIS HARLEY TO PAY THE BANK FOR HIS HOUSE LOAN. IF HE DIDN'T HAVE A WIFE OR KID, HE'D SELL THE HOUSE RATHER THAN THE HARLEY. IN HIS SPARE TIME, HE TENDS TEN OR SO HIVES, BUT THE BEES ARE ILL. EVERYTHING'S GOING TO HELL.

CEDAR RAPIDS

TO TELL THE TRUTH, i REALLY WOULD'VE LIKED TO SEE THE RAPIDS IN CEDAR RAPIDS, BUT YOU CAN'T SEE THEM. i DIDN'T SEE THEM, AT ANY RATE.

 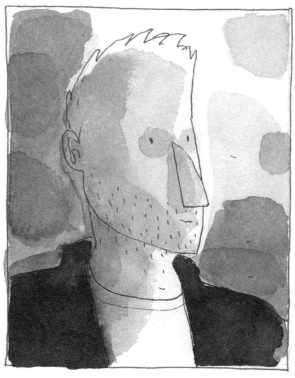

IT'S ALWAYS LIKE THAT. NAMES MAKE US DREAM, AND THEN YOU FEEL A SLIGHT DISAPPOINTMENT. THE MIRACLE IS THAT MY DISAPPOINTMENT DOESN'T DIMINISH THE PLEASURE OF HAVING PASSED BY THERE.

TAMA

COMING OUT OF A BIG CURVE, I SEE A WOODEN CROSS PLANTED ALONGSIDE THE ROAD. A LADY IS DUSTING A WREATH OF ARTIFICIAL FLOWERS. SHE'S A VOLUNTEER TO CLEAN THIS SECTION OF THE ROAD. THE SECRETARY OF THE LINCOLN HIGHWAY ASSOCIATION DIED HERE AT THIS CURVE IN 1920.

BUT THE CROSS WAS PUT IN MEMORY OF EDUARDO, A SIXTEEN-YEAR-OLD BOY WHO WAS KILLED HERE IN 2001. I THANK THE LADY FOR HER EXPLANATION. I SET OFF AGAIN, I RIDE A LITTLE LESS FAST TO AMES.

AMES

BUT, BUT, BUT, i'M iN iOWA AFTER ALL. THE NAME OF "AMES"* iNSPiRES ME TO STOP. THE CAFE BEAUDELAiRE SERVES THREE STAR HAMBURGERS.

* AMES MEANS SOULS IN FRENCH.

AT THE BAR, A GUY'S TALKiNG TO HiMSELF. HE ALTERNATES BETWEEN CONSiDERATiONS ON HiS WiFE AND THE END OF THE WORLD. HE'S WEARiNG A LiFE VEST JUST iN CASE.

MISSOURI VALLEY

AS I EXIT THE CITY, I HAVE A CHOICE: EITHER US 30, WHICH CONTINUES FAITHFULLY STRAIGHT WEST, OR I29, WHICH HEADS DOWN TO SIOUX CITY AND WOULD BE A CHANGE. I HESITATE. US 30 HAS THE ADVANTAGE OF BEING US 30 AND GOING STRAIGHT AHEAD.

INTERSTATE 29 GOES SOUTH TOWARDS A LARGE METRO AREA. I CERTAINLY AM NOT GOING TO FLIP A COIN. THE ABILITY TO CHOOSE IS THE BASIS OF OUR FREEDOM.

LOVELAND

ANY OTHER YEAR, I'D HAVE BEEN HAPPY TO STOP HERE. WITH A NAME LIKE THAT, IT OUGHT TO BE WORTH YOUR WHILE TO GIVE IT A SHOT. I'VE KNOCKED OUT ABOUT 125 MILES SINCE THE CAFE BEAUDELAIRE.

BUT I'M NOT IN THE MOOD. NOT TO MENTION I GOT TO PRESS AHEAD, IF I DON'T WANT TO ARRIVE AT THE BANKS OF THE MISSOURI RIVER TOO LATE.

COUNCIL BLUFFS

I CROSSED IOWA DURING THAT DAY. THINKING BACK ON IT, A BIT OF THE EVENING AT A CASINO WASN'T A WASTE OF TIME. IT'S ALWAYS A FIFTY-FIFTY CHANCE: EITHER YOU WIN OR YOU LOSE. USUALLY I LOSE. BUT YOU NEVER KNOW BEFOREHAND.

THE SLOT MACHINES ARE SPARKLING. THE GUY TO MY RIGHT IS LUCKY. THE COINS KEEP TUMBLING OUT. ON MY LEFT, AN OBESE WOMAN IN A JOGGING SUIT CLUTCHES HER CUP AS THOUGH IT WERE THE HOLY GRAIL, BUT HER CUP'S EMPTYING EVEN FASTER THAN MINE.

THE BRIDGE

WITHOUT REALLY UNDERSTANDING HOW AND UNABLE TO ESCAPE FROM IT, I FIND MYSELF ON A HIGHWAY HEADING SOUTH. SO I'LL ENTER NEBRASKA VIA AN OLD BRIDGE. IN THE MEANTIME, I DON'T GET TIRED OF THE MISSOURI. IT HAS AN AFRICAN AIR. IT'S VERY WIDE AND COVERED WITH MIST.

THE BRIDGE IS BEAUTIFUL, MADE OF STEEL, AND I WONDER HOW MANY RIVETS WERE NEEDED TO ASSEMBLE IT. THE TOWN ACROSS THE WAY BOUGHT IT FOR $1 BEFORE TYING IT BACK TOGETHER. NOW I JUST HAVE TO GO BACK UP THE MISSOURI ON THE OTHER BANK.

OMAHA

SO HERE'S WHERE FRED ASTAIRE WAS BORN. TODAY, I FEEL A LITTLE LIGHTER. ON HIS BIRTH CERTIFICATE, HIS NAME IS FREDERICK AUSTERLITZ. HE'S IN GOOD COMPANY WITH MARLON BRANDO AND MALCOLM X.

THAT SAID, THEY DIDN'T STAY IN OMAHA FOR VERY LONG. I'M JUST PASSING THROUGH MYSELF.

CENTRAL CITY

YOU'D EXPECT A CITY THAT'S ACTUALLY CENTRAL. THE ONLY THING CENTRAL ABOUT IT IS ITS NAME. THERE MUST NOT BE MORE THAN 200 RESIDENTS, AND I DON'T SEE A SINGLE ONE. IT SEEMS THE TOWN WAS FIRST NAMED "ELVIRA." IT WAS THE NAME OF A JUDGE'S WIFE.

NEXT IT WAS CALLED "LONE TREE," BUT THE TWO HUNDRED RESIDENTS OF THE TIME THOUGHT "LONE TREE" WASN'T APPEALING. ONCE PAST THE LAST SHACK, I ACCELERATE. I NEED TO BREATHE.

GRAND ISLAND

THE ROAD CONTINUES TO FOLLOW THE PLATTE RIVER. I CAN CONFIRM THAT THE PLATTE RIVER IS, IN FACT, FLAT.* ON THE OTHER HAND, GRAND ISLAND ISN'T A BIG ISLAND OR A LITTLE ONE. THE CITY ISN'T EVEN LOCATED BESIDE THE WATER. I SPOT THE ORANGE AND BLUE BALL OF A 76 SERVICE STATION.

I GET GAS THERE WHENEVER I CAN, BECAUSE '76 IS THE YEAR OF MY BIRTH. I TAKE THIS CHANCE TO CHECK THE OIL LEVEL. IT'S PERFECT. AFTERWARDS, I CAN'T RESIST A PACK OF CHOCOLATE CHOCOLATE CHIP COOKIES AND THIS WORLD DOESN'T SEEM SO BAD, AFTER ALL. ON THE OTHER HAND, THERE'S NO CAPPUCCINO.

*IN FRENCH, "PLATTE" MEANS "FLAT."

GIBBON

i STOP AT THE GENERAL STORE. THERE'S A TRIKE WITH LEATHER STRIPS ON THE HANDLEBARS IN THE PARKING LOT. INSIDE THE STORE, THE BIKERS ARE EACH AT LEAST SEVENTY YEARS OLD. THEY'VE BOUGHT TWO CANS OF 7 UP. HER HAIR IS COLORED GREEN. HE LIMPS. HE HAS AN ARTIFICIAL LEG.

HE LOST HIS REAL ONE IN VIETNAM. SO, THE TRIKE HAS SAVED HIM FROM TOO MUCH OF THE BLUES. i FIND MY CAPPUCCINO. AT $2.99, THE PRICE IS RIGHT. THE THREE OF US CLINK CUPS IN THE PARKING LOT FACING THE EMPTY EXPANSE OF THE PRAIRIE.

NORTH PLATTE

THE MOTEL RESEMBLES EVERY MOTEL. IN THE BAR BESIDE THE HOTEL, AN OLD JUKEBOX IS BLINKING UNDER A BIG PICTURE OF THE SIOUX CHIEF RED CLOUD, WHO WAS BORN IN NORTH PLATTE. THE LOCALS ARE PLAYING FIDDLE AND BANJO TUNES.

I SLIP A QUARTER INTO THE SLOT TO HEAR "MY WAY." THE EVENING PASSES BY WITH AN INFINITE GENTLENESS. BEFORE GOING BACK TO MY ROOM, I SIT ON THE SIDEWALK ALONGSIDE THE ROAD. I LIGHT A CIGARETTE AND WATCH THE SEMIS PASS BY.

OGALLALA

EVER SINCE THE ROAD BEGAN RUNNING ALONGSIDE A TRAIN TRACK, I WAS BOUND TO OVERTAKE OR CROSS PATHS WITH A TRAIN. DONE. I CAUGHT UP WITH IT. I SLOWED TO ROLL ALONG AT THE SAME SPEED AND TRIED TO GUESS WHAT MERCHANDISE IT WAS CARRYING.

I COUNTED 106 CARS, BUT I WON'T GUARANTEE ANYTHING. IT MAY HAVE BEEN 107 OR 105. I KEPT AN EYE ON IT IN THE REARVIEW MIRROR UNTIL IT DISAPPEARED.

KIMBALL

IN THE DISTANCE, YOU CAN SEE THE BARRIER OF THE ROCKY MOUNTAINS. YOU SEE IT FOR A LONG TIME, EVEN WHILE DRIVING FAST. AT THIS PACE, i WON'T AVOID A SHORT SPELL OF NiGHTTiME DRiViNG.

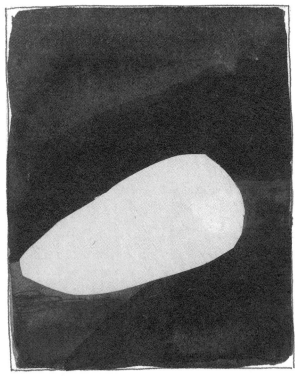

BUT i LOVE iT: THE PAiNTBRUSH OF THE HEADLIGHT, THE DARKNESS ALL AROUND, THE SENSATION OF FLYiNG. i JUST HAVE TO BE A LiTTLE MORE ATTENTiVE.

CHEYENNE

THAT'S IT, I'M THERE! IN THE WEST. I'VE STOPPED COUNTING RODEO SIGNS. I
ORDER A T-BONE IN A CROWDED STEAKHOUSE; AT THE NEIGHBORING TABLE, JOE
WAVES ME OVER TO COME TRY THE HONEY WHISKEY.

I DON'T KNOW WHY, BUT I LIKE HIM. BEFORE WE PART, HE TELLS ME I CAN SLEEP
OVER AT HIS BROTHER'S PLACE IN SAN FRANCISCO. HE WRITES DOWN THE ADDRESS
FOR ME ON A PIECE OF PAPER. IT'S SIMPLE, YOU'LL SEE. THERE ARE FOUR MEXICAN
FAN PALM TREES WITH SKINNY TRUNKS AT THE END OF THE STREET.

THE FOLLOWING MORNING, I PASS IN FRONT OF THE GIANT SANTIAGS OF THE UNION PACIFIC DEPOT. NOT FAR, THERE'S THE WRANGLER BUILDING. THEY BUY AND SELL JEANS, SHIRTS, JACKETS, BOOTS AND BELTS. I DON'T HAVE ROOM ON THE BIKE. SO I JUST SETTLE FOR A YELLOW BELT. APPARENTLY, IT'S OSTRIDGE.

THE SALESWOMAN HAS AN OLIVE COMPLEXION, BLACK HAIR OVER HER NECK, AND SHE GETS OFF THIS EVENING AT 10PM. I'D GLADLY SPEND TWO NIGHTS IN CHEYENNE AFTER ALL.

TREE ROCK SHERMAN HILL

THIS MORNING, I ATTACK THE ROCKIES. I'M ON US 30 BECAUSE THE ORIGINAL ROAD HAS BEEN ABANDONED. GRASS IS GROWING BETWEEN THE SLABS OF POTHOLED TARMAC. AT ONE MOMENT, YOU PASS IN FRONT OF A TREE BETWEEN BLOCKS OF PINK GRANITE,

PROTECTED BY A FENCE LIKE IN A BOTANICAL GARDEN. IT WAS THERE ALREADY WHEN THE FIRST PIONEERS BLAZED THEIR TRAIL. IT'S A PINE. THE ROAD CLIMBS AND TURNS. THAT'S A CHANGE. NO WIND. IT'S EASY TO KEEP CONTROL OF THE BIKE.

COMO BLUFFS

A SIGN INVITES US ON A SLIGHT DETOUR TO ADMIRE A HOUSE BUILT FROM SIX THOUSAND DINOSAUR BONES. I JUST COULDN'T MISS THAT. IT TURNS OUT THERE ARE ONLY 5,796 BONES. THE HOUSE ISN'T IMPRESSIVE AT ALL, EVEN WHEN YOU GET CLOSER, IT LOOKS LIKE LOGS.

THEY WERE RAILROAD WORKERS WHO DUG INTO A DINOSAUR CEMETERY. IN THE FALL, THE HOUSE IS CLOSED, BUT THE IMPORTANT THING IS TO SEE IT FROM THE OUTSIDE.

"I REMEMBER JUST HOW THOSE MEN LOOKED AS WE RODE UP THE LITTLE HILL WHERE THEIR CAMP WAS. THE RED LIGHT OF THE MORNING SUN WAS STREAMING UPON THEM AS THEY LAY, HEADS TOWARDS US, ON THE GROUND, AND EVERY MAN HAD A ROUND RED SPOT ON TOP OF HIS HEAD, ABOUT AS BIG AS A DOLLAR WHERE THE REDSKINS HAD TAKEN HIS SCALP. IT WAS FRIGHTFUL, BUT IT WAS GROTESQUE, AND THE RED SUNLIGHT SEEMED TO PAINT EVERYTHING ALL OVER."

WAMSUTTER

THE BROADWAY CAFE IS A LITTLE CUBE PAINTED SKY-BLUE AND WHITE, SITTING BESIDE THE ROAD, WITH PLEATED DRAPES ON THE WINDOWS, THE STARS AND STRIPES BESIDE THE ENTRANCE, A WATER TOWER ACROSS THE WAY, WITH SUNNYSIDE UP EGGS TO DIE FOR, AND THE BEST COFFEE.

BEYOND IT IS THE RED DESERT, WHOSE DUNES AREN'T RED YET AT THIS HOUR, A BYGONE LAKE WHOSE WATER EVAPORATED, WITH IMMENSE DEPOSITS OF URANIUM. I STILL HAVE ABOUT 200 MILES TO GO UNTIL THE UTAH STATE LINE.

SALT LAKE CITY

IT'S A BIG CITY SET IN THE MIDDLE OF THE DESERT. MOST OF ITS RESIDENTS ARE MORMONS. THEY'RE FRIENDLY, BUT THERE'S SOMETHING ODD ABOUT THEIR APPEARANCE. JUST THAT NAME: THE CHURCH OF JESUS CHRIST OF THE LATTER-DAY SAINTS.

THEY USED TO BE POLYGAMOUS. SOME STILL ARE. HOW DO THEY DO MANAGE? I HAD ONLY ONE WOMAN, AND SHE DUMPED ME.

THE HOTEL MANAGER INTRODUCES HER BROTHER TO ME. HE'S OF AN INDETERMINATE AGE, SITTING ON A PLASTIC CHAIR IN FRONT OF A 90 SQUARE FOOT INDOOR POOL. IN FACT, HE'S 30. HIS LIFE'S BEEN A WRECK EVER SINCE HE FOUND A JOB CLEANING UP AN OIL SLICK AFTER A HUGE LEAK OFFSHORE.

SINCE THEN, HE WALKS AROUND LIKE AN OLD MAN AND, ALTHOUGH HE SPEAKS WITH DIFFICULTY, HE SAYS THE ESSENTIAL: "I FEEL LIKE MY BRAIN'S BEEN FRIED. I GET LOST IN MY OWN YARD. I CAN'T DRIVE ANYMORE. I CAN'T EVEN TAKE CARE OF MY KIDS NOW."

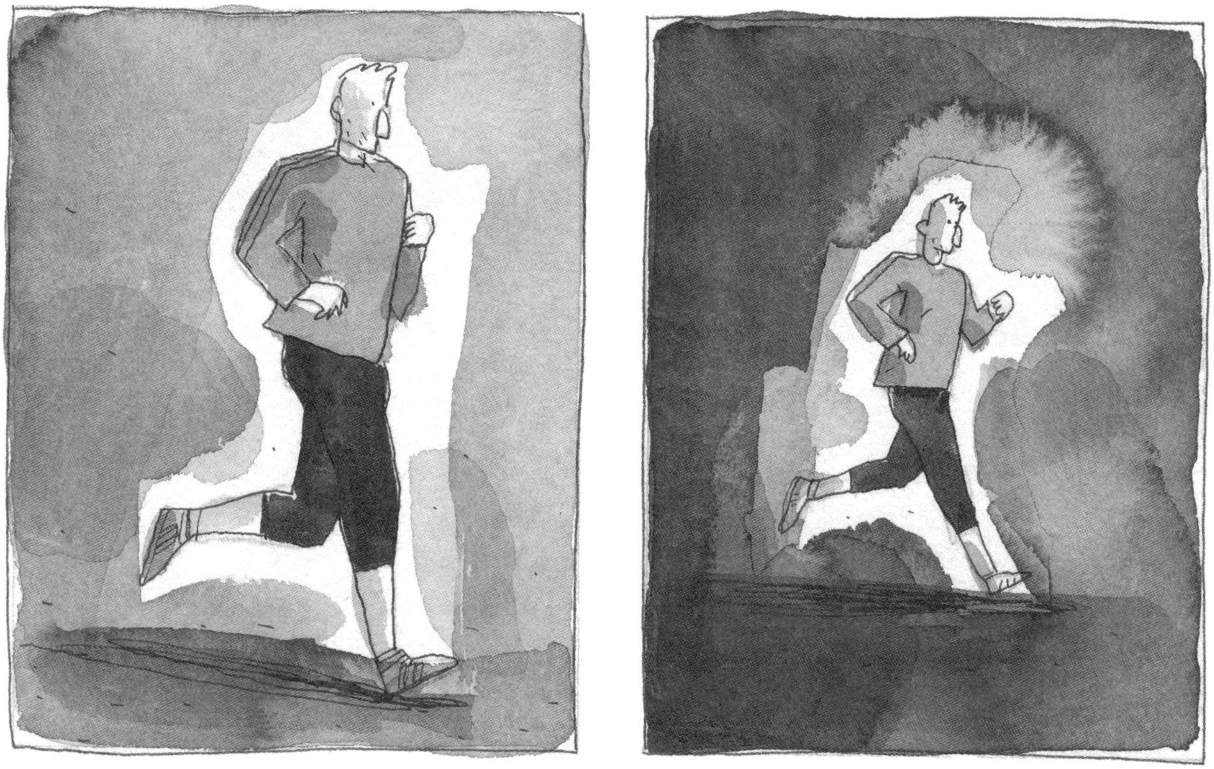

SUDDENLY, I DON'T HESITATE A SECOND LONGER. I'M GONNA RUN! I HEAD DOWN TOWARDS THE PLANETARIUM, FACING THE SUN WHICH WILL BE SETTING SOON. IT'S LIKE I'M IN FRONT OF A POSTCARD.

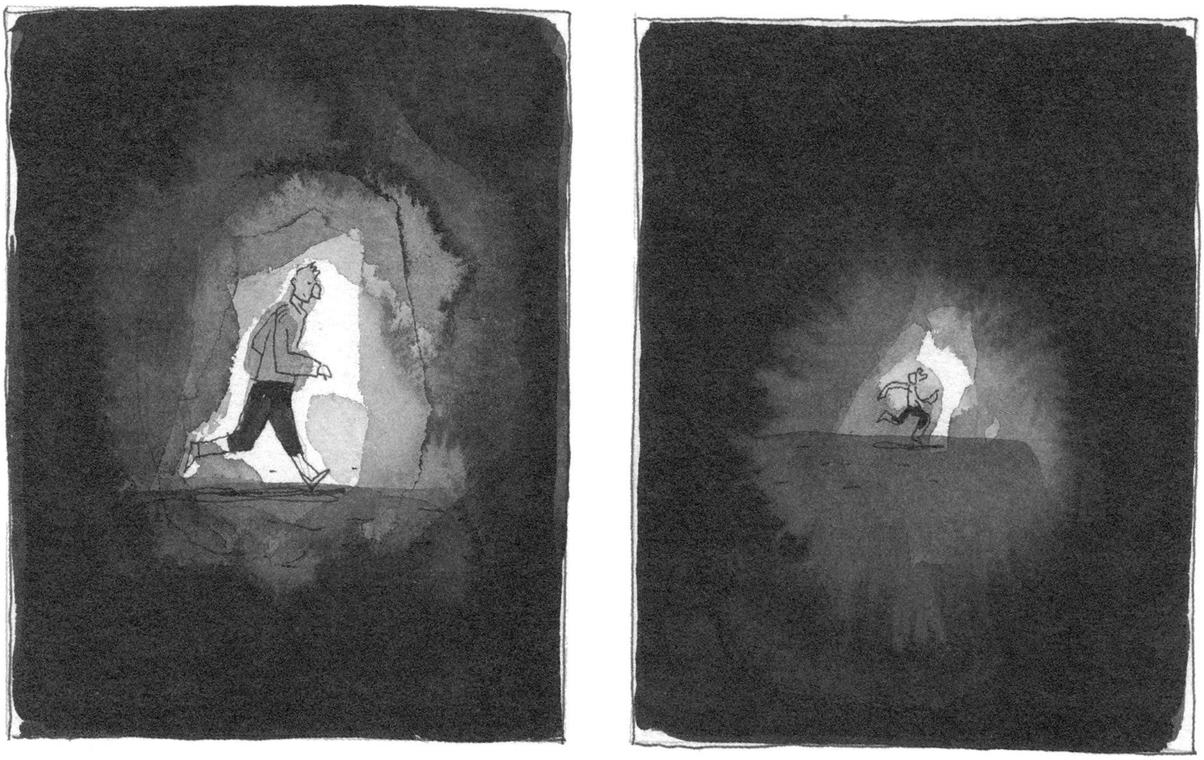

I RUN FOR MORE THAN AN HOUR. I FEEL GOOD.

THE GREAT SALT LAKE

YOU CAN SEE IT FROM FAR AWAY OVER THE LAKE. THE TREE OF LIFE STANDS 87 FEET TALL. IT'S A GIANT SCULPTURE. WHEN YOU GET CLOSER, YOU REALIZE ITS LEAVES ARE BALLS OF STONE.

MOTORBIKE SPEED RACING TAKES PLACE FROM AUGUST TO OCTOBER OVER THAT WAY. IT SEEMS SOME GUY RODE FASTER THAN 370 MPH. I LEAVE THE TREE OF LIFE BEHIND. I MAY NOT BE GOING FAST, BUT I HAVE MILES TO GO.

WENDOVER

WENDOVER IS IN UTAH, STILL. WEST WENDOVER IS IN NEVADA ALREADY.

I TURN MY WATCH BACK ONE HOUR AND, TO CELEBRATE THE OCCASION, I DRIVE UP A PEAK AT 120MPH.

HORIZON VIEW POINT

I'M ON US 50. THE "HORIZON VIEW POINT" SIGN PERFECTLY SUMS UP THE SITUATION. YEP. IT'S BREATHTAKING.

BUT, FRANKLY, THE LANDSCAPE IS SO VAST YOU COULD'VE PUT THE SIGN ANYWHERE.

EUREKA

YOU GOTTA GET LUCKY FROM TIME TO TIME. i WAS. i LIKE EUREKA. IN THE DOWNTOWN, THERE'S A BIG BUILDING MADE OF RASPBERRY RED BRICKS THAT MATCHES THE GRAY OF THE SKY. iT'S AN OPERA HOUSE. iT DATES FROM 1879.

THE MOTEL iS SIMPLE. THE RESTAURANT WAITRESS iS WEARING A BRAND NEW "i SURVIVED" TEE-SHIRT. SHE HAS MINT SYRUP EYES AND A MEZZO VOICE. i COULD'VE LISTENED TO HER ALL NIGHT LONG.

"i SURVIVED" HAS TODAY OFF. SHE SLIPPED ON AN APPLE GREEN SWEATSHIRT AND ASKED ME IF I CAN DROP HER OFF AT HER SISTER'S IN AUSTIN, UT. AFTER WHAT SHE TOLD ME YESTERDAY, i CAN'T SAY NO.

SHE'S USED TO MOTORCYCLES. i'M FLUSTERED FROM FEELING HER ARMS AROUND MY WAIST. i ACCELERATE SLOWLY. SHE LAYS HER HEAD AGAINST MY SHOULDER, AND iT'S LiKE THE WORLD SUDDENLY STOPPED TURNING.

MIDDLEGATE, SHOE TREE

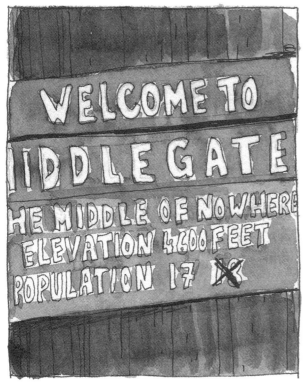

THE TREE IS A POPLAR. ITS LEAVES ARE YELLOWING. DOZENS AND DOZENS OF SHOES ARE HANGING ON ITS BRANCHES. THERE ARE ALL KINDS OF THEM, GENERALLY IN PAIRS, BUT NOT NECESSARILY. TENNIS SHOES, SANDALS, BOOTS, CHUKKA BOOTS, AND HIGH HEELS,

BALLET SHOES, MOCCASINS, ROLLERBLADES, AND ICE SKATES EVEN, ALL OF THEM HAVING A STORY, A GOOD REASON TO BE SUSPENDED HERE ON THE BRANCHES OF A POPLAR IN THE MIDDLE OF THE DESERT. IF I UNDERSTOOD RIGHT, IT'S A BIT LIKE THE THING WITH PADLOCKS ON PARIS' PONT DES ARTS.

RENO

i DIDN'T DO THIS DELIBERATELY. RENO USED TO BE FAMOUS FOR BEING THE CITY WHERE PEOPLE GOT DIVORCED. NOW, PEOPLE GET DIVORCED EVERYWHERE. RENO IS ALSO THE CITY WHERE YOU CAN GET MARRIED OR REMARRIED AT A DRIVE-THRU, WITHOUT GETTING OUT OF YOUR CAR, FOR $20, OR AN ADDITIONAL $10, IF YOU WANT A WITNESS,

WITH A FEW OPTIONS LIKE THE GLASS OF CHAMPAGNE OR SPECIAL HONEYMOON LINGERIE. i DON'T FEEL LIKE GOING BACK TO GO TO BED. i MEANDER, MY HANDS IN THE POCKETS OF MY LEATHER JACKET. IT'S STARTING TO GET COLD.

SO THIS IS THE FINAL STAGE OF THE CROSSING. THIS MORNING, IT'S CHILLY. THE SKY IS CLEAR. THE MAP SHOWS THAT THE LINCOLN HIGHWAY DIVIDES INTO TWO. TWO ROUTES ARE POSSIBLE: TO THE NORTH THROUGH EMIGRANT GAP AND GOLD RUN, TO THE SOUTH VIA STRAWBERRY AND POLLOCK PINES. WHICH ONE DO I CHOOSE?

TODAY I FLIP A COIN. THAT'S LOGICAL IN THE LAND OF GAMBLING.

LAKE TAHOE

THE LAKE IS A DEEP BLUE. MAKES SENSE SINCE IT'S 1500 FEET DEEP. AND IT'S TWO MILLION YEARS OLD. I START THE DESCENT THROUGH THE PINES. I'M GOING SLOWLY. I LET THE BIKE ROLL. I ONLY APPLY THE GAS AROUND BENDS,

BUT I IMMEDIATELY LET UP BECAUSE THE TRIP IS ALMOST FINISHED AND I WANT TO SAVOR EVERY SECOND. I TAKE OFF MY HELMET, HANG IT ON THE BACK OF MY SEAT AND SLIDE INTO THE SOFTNESS OF THE AMBIENT AIR.

"IF I AM KILLED, I CAN
DIE BUT ONCE; BUT TO
LIVE IN CONSTANT DREAD
OF IT, IS TO DIE OVER
AND OVER AGAIN."

BERKELEY

i DON'T KNOW HOW MANY BRIDGES i'VE CROSSED BEFORE ARRIVING, BUT i ARRIVED. i PARK THE SHADOW 750 iN FRONT OF JOE'S BROTHER'S HOUSE.

AT THE END OF HILLEGASS AVENUE, THERE ARE FOUR MEXICAN FAN PALM TREES WiTH SKiNNY LONG TRUNKS STANDING WATCH. i'M GOiNG TO RUN THAT EVENiNG. FOR THE FIRST TIME IN A LONG WHiLE, i RUN FOR TWO HOURS. EFFORTLESSLY. WiTH PLEASURE.

SAN FRANCISCO

IT'S FUNNY HOW YOU CAN KNOW A CITY WHERE YOU'VE NEVER SET FOOT. I FEEL LIKE I RECOGNIZE THE STEEP STREETS, THE SHOPS IN THE CHINESE, ITALIAN, AND MEXICAN NEIGHBORHOODS. IN A GOODWILL STORE, I BUY MYSELF TWO WHITE, COTTON SHIRTS FOR $10 (FOR BOTH).

AT A BOOTH, I BUY THREE POSTCARDS OF THE GOLDEN GATE BRIDGE UNDER THE SETTING SUN. ONE FOR JOE IN CHEYENNE, ONE FOR NAT IN PITTSBURGH, AND ONE FOR ED IN NEW YORK. THE ONLY PROBLEM IS THAT I DON'T HAVE ED'S ADDRESS.

POTEAU TERMINUS, LINCOLN HIGHWAY

I LET MYSELF GO DOWN TO FISHERMAN'S WHARF. YOU CAN ADMIRE THE SEALS FOR FREE AND CROSS THE BAY FOR A HANDFUL OF DOLLARS. IN THE MEANTIME, I BUY A (PAPER) PLATE OF CALAMARI AND A BEER (IN A CUP).

OUT OF IDLENESS, I GO INTO THE MUSEE MECANIQUE ARCADE WHERE CHANCE BRINGS ME IN FRONT OF A LOVE TESTER MACHINE THAT'S BLINKING LIKE A CHRISTMAS TREE. I WON'T SLINK AWAY, I TAKE THE TEST.

I CAN FINALLY ANSWER MY GIRLFRIEND'S TEXT MESSAGE. GAME OVER.

AT THE EXIT, i WALK FOR ANOTHER HOUR ALONG THE WHARF, TOWARDS LINCOLN BOULEVARD. THEN i SiT DOWN ON A BENCH, FACiNG THE OCEAN AND, i SUPPOSE, JAPAN.

THE END

Lincoln Highway

Throughout these weeks spent on the road, the narrator crossed many states and discovered, far from the legendary Route 66, another America. The main stages of his ride are indicated on the map below.

WYOMING

NEVADA

NEBRASKA

UTAH

COLORADO

KANSAS

CALIFORNIA

① **Verrazzano Bridge,** New York
② **Manhattan,** New York
③ **Hudson River,** New York
④ **Weehawken,** New Jersey
⑤ **Princeton,** New Jersey
⑥ **Trenton,** New Jersey
⑦ **Langhorne,** Pennsylvania
⑧ **Philadelphia,** Pennsylvania
⑨ **Paradise,** Pennsylvania

⑩ **Gettysburg,** Pennsylvania
⑪ **Fayetteville,** Pennsylvania
⑫ **Turtle Creek,** Pennsylvania
⑬ **Pittsburgh,** Pennsylvania
⑭ **East Liverpool,** Ohio
⑮ **Canton,** Ohio
⑯ **Van Wert,** Ohio
⑰ **Zulu,** Indiana
⑱ **Fort Wayne,** Indiana

⑲ **Chicago,** Illinois
⑳ **Plainfield,** Illinois
㉑ **DeKalb,** Illinois
㉒ **Clinton,** Illinois
㉓ **Cesar Rapids,** Iowa
㉔ **Tama,** Iowa
㉕ **Ames,** Iowa
㉖ **Missouri Valley,** Iowa
㉗ **Council Bluffs,** Iowa

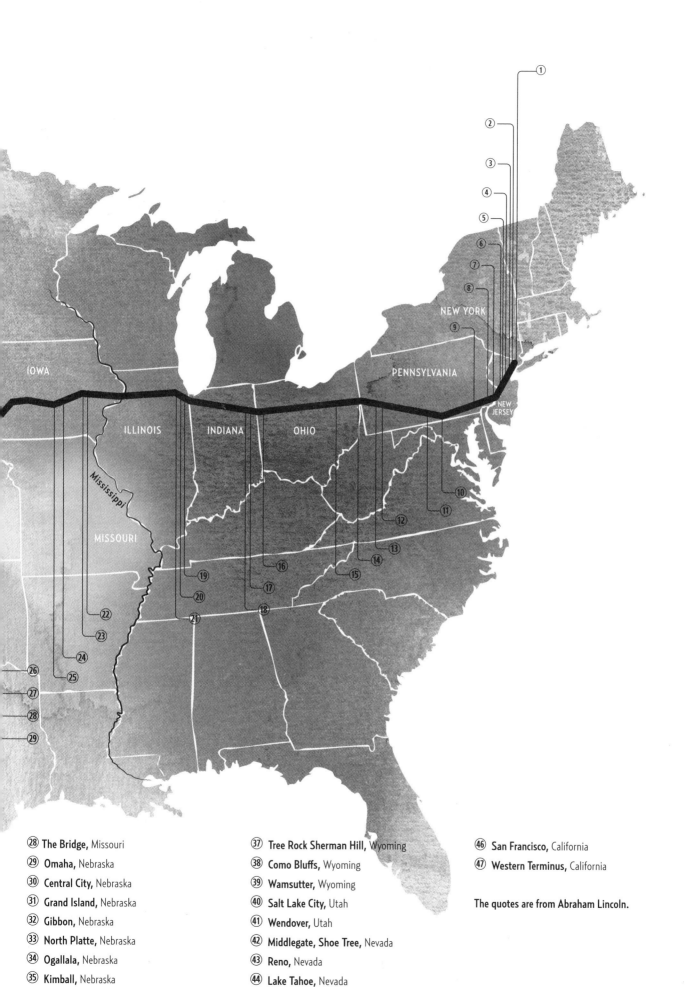

28 **The Bridge,** Missouri

29 **Omaha,** Nebraska

30 **Central City,** Nebraska

31 **Grand Island,** Nebraska

32 **Gibbon,** Nebraska

33 **North Platte,** Nebraska

34 **Ogallala,** Nebraska

35 **Kimball,** Nebraska

36 **Cheyenne,** Wyoming

37 **Tree Rock Sherman Hill,** Wyoming

38 **Como Bluffs,** Wyoming

39 **Wamsutter,** Wyoming

40 **Salt Lake City,** Utah

41 **Wendover,** Utah

42 **Middlegate, Shoe Tree,** Nevada

43 **Reno,** Nevada

44 **Lake Tahoe,** Nevada

45 **Berkeley,** California

46 **San Francisco,** California

47 **Western Terminus,** California

The quotes are from Abraham Lincoln.

Also available from NBM Graphic Novels:

Silent Invasion, series of 4, Michael Cherkas & Larry Hancock

"Like the greatest episodes of "The Twilight Zone," "The Silent Invasion"
mashes together the earthbound fears of a particular time with a threat
from the outside to make an argument about the world around us."
- **William Kulesa, NJ.com/Jersey Journal**

The Initiates, by Etienne Davodeau

A winemaker exchanges jobs with a comic artist

A Publishers Weekly Critics Poll Selection

The Broadcast by Eric Hobbs & Noel Tuazon

"Intriguing character study of different personalities under pressure.
Tuazon's art adds to the ominous mood." **-Publishers Weekly**

We have hundreds of graphic novels.
See them all at:
NBMPUB.COM

NBM
160 Broadway, Suite 700, East Wing,
New York, NY 10038
Catalog upon request

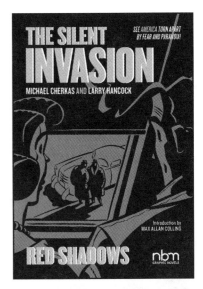

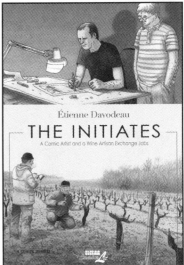